Christmas Favorites

For Piano
Compiled, Arranged and Edited by
Wesley Schaum

For Beginners of All Ages with Words and Illustrations

Foreword

This book is planned to provide both adults and children with an appealing selection of familiar Christmas music, both sacred and secular. The pieces are grouped in order of increasing difficulty, so that this album might be used to parallel a method book. This grouping also serves to sustain interest and provide a gradual challenge while progressing through the book.

Finger numbers are purposely kept at a minimum, only the essentials, so that note reading is encouraged. Key signatures have been omitted for sake of simplicity; complicated rhythms have been avoided. Effort has been made to maintain the five-finger position and to give approximately equal work to each hand. Although only the first verse of most songs has been included, additional verses may, of course be used.

The duet accompaniments(obviously, not at the same level as the melody) may be played by teacher, parent, older student, or another person and are intended to provide rhythmic training, ensemble experience and opportunities for recital performance, if desired. The person playing the accompaniment is free to add pedal according to personal taste.

Exclusively Distributed By

HAL•LEONARD®
C O R P O R A T I O N
7777 W. BLUEMOUND RD. P.O. BOX 13819 MILWAUKEE, WI 53213

Index

Schaum Christmas Tree Award

TEACHER'S NOTE: The Schaum Christmas Tree Award page is intended to trace the progress of the student thru this book. If desired, the student may paste a star on this page as he finishes each piece. The stars of the tree are numbered to correspond with the title numbers of each piece. The reverse side of this page is blank so it may be removed from the book without damage to the contents. When the book is completed, the student may cut out this page and frame it, or attach it to a bulletin board or wall.

1. Toyland

Glen MacDonough *

Victor Herbert *

Allegretto

mp Toy - land! Toy - land! Dear lit - tle girl and

boy land. While you dwell with - in it

you are ev - er hap - py then.____

ACCOMPANIMENT

*Note to students: The author of the words has his name placed above the music on the left-hand side. The composer of the music is placed on the right-hand side. If there is no name on the left-hand side, it is assumed that the same person wrote both words and music.

2. I Saw Three Ships

Traditional English

Allegretto

mf I saw three ships come sail - ing

in, On Christ - mas Day, on Christ - mas Day; I saw three

ships come sail - ing in, On Christ - mas Day in the morn - ing.

ACCOMPANIMENT*

*The person playing the accompaniment is free to add pedal according to his own taste.

3. Good King Wenceslas

Old English Carol

Allegretto

Good King Wen - ces - las look'd out On the Feast of Ste - phen,

When the snow lay 'round a - bout, Deep and crisp, and e - ven:

Bright - ly shone the moon that night, Tho' the frost was cru - el,

When a poor man came in sight, Gath-'ring win - ter fu - el.

ACCOMPANIMENT

4. We Three Kings of Orient Are

J. H. Hopkins

night, Star with roy - al beau - ty

bright; West - ward lead - ing, still pro -

ceed - ing, Guide us to thy per - fect light.

ACCOMPANIMENT (continued)

5. Jolly Old St. Nicholas

Traditional

Allegretto

mf

Jol - ly old Saint Nich - o - las, Lean your ear this way! Don't you tell a

sin - gle soul What I'm going to say; Christ-mas Eve is com - ing soon;

Now, you dear old man, Whis-per what you'll bring to me; Tell me if you can.

ACCOMPANIMENT

6. O Come, Little Children

C. von Schmidt

J. A. P. Schulz

7. It Came Upon the Midnight Clear

Edmund H. Sears

Richard S. Willis

ACCOMPANIMENT

men From heav — en's all gra — cious King, ____

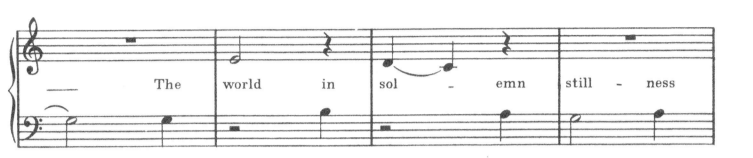

____ The world in sol — emn still — ness

lay To hear the an — gels sing. ____

ACCOMPANIMENT (continued)

8. O Come All Ye Faithful

Latin, 18th Century

J. F. Wade

Andantino

mf O come, all ye faith-ful, Joy-ful and tri-um-phant; O come ye, O come ye to Beth - le - hem; Come and be-hold Him, Born the King of an - gels; O come, let us a-dore Him, O come, let us a-dore Him, O come, let us a-dore Him,__ Christ__ the Lord.

ACCOMPANIMENT

9. O Little Town of Bethlehem

Phillips Brooks

Lewis H. Redner

Andantino

mp O lit-tle town of Beth-le-hem, How still we see thee lie! A-

bove thy deep and dream-less sleep The si-lent stars go by. Yet

in thy dark streets shin-eth the ev-er-last-ing Light; The

hopes and fears of all the years Are met in thee to-night.

ACCOMPANIMENT

10. Over the River and Thru the Wood

Early American Song

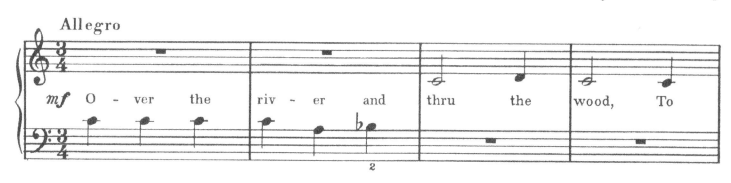

Allegro

mf O - ver the riv - er and thru the wood, To

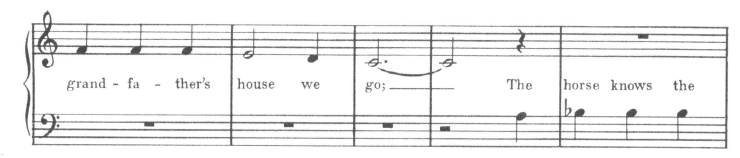

grand - fa - ther's house we go; ___ The horse knows the

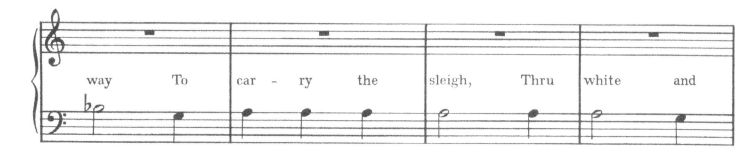

way To car - ry the sleigh, Thru white and

ACCOMPANIMENT

drift - ed   snow._____   O - ver the   riv - er and

thru   the   wood,   Oh,   how   the   wind   does

blow!_____   It   stings   the   toes,   and   bites   the

nose,   As   o - ver the   ground   we   go._____

ACCOMPANIMENT (continued)

11. Winds Thru the Olive Trees

Traditional

Andante

Winds thru the ol - ive trees

soft - ly did blow; 'Round lit - tle Beth-le-hem Long, long a - go. Sheep on the

hill-side lay whit-er than snow, Shep-herds were watch-ing them, Long, long a - go.

ACCOMPANIMENT

TEACHER'S NOTE: If the pupil is in the early grades in school and has not had fractions, do not attempt to explain the dotted quarter notes and rests. The rule to follow is this: EXPERIENCE SHOULD PRECEDE EXPLANATION. Teach the rhythm by rote. Delay the explanation until the problem arises at a later time when the pupil has acquired fraction readiness.

12. Away in a Manger

German Children's Carol

ACCOMPANIMENT

13. Jingle Bells

J. Pierpont

Allegro

mf

Jin-gle bells! Jin-gle bells! Jin-gle all the way! Oh, what fun it

is to ride In a one horse o-pen sleigh!__ Jin-gle bells! Jin-gle bells!

Jin-gle all the way! Oh, what fun it is to ride In a one horse o-pen sleigh!

Play one octave higher throughout.

ACCOMPANIMENT

14. Up on the Housetop

B. R. Hanby

15. Silent Night

Franz Gruber

ACCOMPANIMENT

16. I Heard the Bells on Christmas Day

Henry W. Longfellow

J. Baptiste Calkin

Andante

I heard the bells on Christ - mas Day, Their old fa - mil - iar car - ols play, And wild and sweet the words re - peat Of peace on earth, good will to men.

Play all notes of accompaniment
one octave higher throughout

ACCOMPANIMENT

17. Hark! The Herald Angels Sing

Charles Wesley

Felix Mendelssohn

ACCOMPANIMENT

18. What Child is This?

(Greensleeves)

Old English

Adagio

What Child is this,— Who laid to rest— On Mar - y's

lap — is sleep - ing? Whom an - gels greet — with

an - thems sweet,— While shep - herds watch — are keep - ing?

ACCOMPANIMENT

19. We Wish You a Merry Christmas

Traditional English

20. O Christmas Tree

(O Tannenbaum)

German Folk Melody

ACCOMPANIMENT

TEACHER'S NOTE: If desired, a ♩. ♪ rhythm may be substituted for ♪♪ rhythm in this piece. It is suggested that the ♩. ♪ rhythm be taught by rote.

21. While Shepherds Watched Their Flocks

Nahum Tate

G. F. Handel

ACCOMPANIMENT

22. Joy to the World

Isaac Watts

G. F. Handel

Allegretto

f Joy to the world! The Lord is come; Let earth re-

ceive her King; Let ev-'ry heart pre-

pare him room, And heav'n and na-ture sing, And

heav'n and na-ture sing, And heav-en and heav-en and na-ture sing.

ACCOMPANIMENT

23. The First Noel

Traditional

24. Deck the Hall

Traditional Welsh